Everything You Ever Wanted to Know About Dallas Cowboys

© 2017 Ian Carroll

Everything You Ever Wanted to Know About....

Absolutely nothing, because we really don't care...

Everything You Ever Wanted to Know About...

Absolutely nothing, because we really don't care...

Everything You Ever Wanted to Know About...

Absolutely nothing, because we really don't care...

Everything You Ever Wanted to Know About...

Absolutely nothing, because we really don't care...

Everything You Ever Wanted to Know About...

Absolutely nothing, because we really don't care...

Everything You Ever Wanted to Know About...

Absolutely nothing, because we really don't care...

Everything You Ever Wanted to Know About...

Absolutely nothing, because we really don't care...

Everything You Ever Wanted to Know About...

Absolutely nothing, because we really don't care...

Everything You Ever Wanted to Know About...

Absolutely nothing, because we really don't care...

Everything You Ever Wanted to Know About...

Absolutely nothing, because we really don't care...

Everything You Ever Wanted to Know About...

Absolutely nothing, because we really don't care...

Everything You Ever Wanted to Know About...

Absolutely nothing, because we really don't care....

Everything You Ever Wanted to Know About....

Absolutely nothing, because we really don't care...

Everything You Ever Wanted to Know About...

Absolutely nothing, because we really don't care…..

Everything You Ever Wanted to Know About…..

Absolutely nothing, because we really don't care…

Everything You Ever Wanted to Know About...

Absolutely nothing, because we really don't care...

Everything You Ever Wanted to Know About...

Absolutely nothing, because we really don't care...

Everything You Ever Wanted to Know About...

Absolutely nothing, because we really don't care...

Everything You Ever Wanted to Know About...

Absolutely nothing, because we really don't care...

Everything You Ever Wanted to Know About...

Absolutely nothing, because we really don't care...

Everything You Ever Wanted to Know About...

Absolutely nothing, because we really don't care...

Everything You Ever Wanted to Know About...

Absolutely nothing, because we really don't care...

Everything You Ever Wanted to Know About...

Absolutely nothing, because we really don't care...

Everything You Ever Wanted to Know About...

Absolutely nothing, because we really don't care...

Everything You Ever Wanted to Know About...

Absolutely nothing, because we really don't care...

Everything You Ever Wanted to Know About...

Absolutely nothing, because we really don't care...

Everything You Ever Wanted to Know About...

Absolutely nothing, because we really don't care...

Everything You Ever Wanted to Know About…

Absolutely nothing, because we really don't care…

Everything You Ever Wanted to Know About...

Absolutely nothing, because we really don't care...

Everything You Ever Wanted to Know About...

Absolutely nothing, because we really don't care...

Everything You Ever Wanted to Know About...

Absolutely nothing, because we really don't care...

Everything You Ever Wanted to Know About...

Absolutely nothing, because we really don't care...

Everything You Ever Wanted to Know About...

Absolutely nothing, because we really don't care...

Everything You Ever Wanted to Know About...

Absolutely nothing, because we really don't care....

Everything You Ever Wanted to Know About....

Absolutely nothing, because we really don't care...

Everything You Ever Wanted to Know About...

Absolutely nothing, because we really don't care...

Everything You Ever Wanted to Know About...

Absolutely nothing, because we really don't care...

Everything You Ever Wanted to Know About...

Absolutely nothing, because we really don't care...

Everything You Ever Wanted to Know About...

Absolutely nothing, because we really don't care...

Everything You Ever Wanted to Know About....

Absolutely nothing, because we really don't care...

Everything You Ever Wanted to Know About….

Absolutely nothing, because we really don't care…

Everything You Ever Wanted to Know About...

Absolutely nothing, because we really don't care...

Everything You Ever Wanted to Know About...

Absolutely nothing, because we really don't care...

Everything You Ever Wanted to Know About...

Absolutely nothing, because we really don't care...

Everything You Ever Wanted to Know About...

Absolutely nothing, because we really don't care...

Everything You Ever Wanted to Know About...

Absolutely nothing, because we really don't care…..

Everything You Ever Wanted to Know About…..

Absolutely nothing, because we really don't care…

Everything You Ever Wanted to Know About...

Absolutely nothing, because we really don't care...

Everything You Ever Wanted to Know About…

Absolutely nothing, because we really don't care…

Everything You Ever Wanted to Know About...

Absolutely nothing, because we really don't care...

Everything You Ever Wanted to Know About...

Absolutely nothing, because we really don't care...

Everything You Ever Wanted to Know About...

Absolutely nothing, because we really don't care...

Everything You Ever Wanted to Know About...

Absolutely nothing, because we really don't care...

Everything You Ever Wanted to Know About...

Absolutely nothing, because we really don't care...

Everything You Ever Wanted to Know About...

Absolutely nothing, because we really don't care...

Everything You Ever Wanted to Know About...

Absolutely nothing, because we really don't care...

Everything You Ever Wanted to Know About...

Absolutely nothing, because we really don't care...

Everything You Ever Wanted to Know About...

Absolutely nothing, because we really don't care....

Everything You Ever Wanted to Know About…..

Absolutely nothing, because we really don't care…

Everything You Ever Wanted to Know About…

Absolutely nothing, because we really don't care…

Everything You Ever Wanted to Know About...

Absolutely nothing, because we really don't care....

Everything You Ever Wanted to Know About...

Absolutely nothing, because we really don't care...

Everything You Ever Wanted to Know About...

Absolutely nothing, because we really don't care...

Everything You Ever Wanted to Know About...

Absolutely nothing, because we really don't care...

Everything You Ever Wanted to Know About...

Absolutely nothing, because we really don't care...

Everything You Ever Wanted to Know About...

Absolutely nothing, because we really don't care....

Everything You Ever Wanted to Know About....

Absolutely nothing, because we really don't care...

Everything You Ever Wanted to Know About...

Absolutely nothing, because we really don't care...

Everything You Ever Wanted to Know About...

Absolutely nothing, because we really don't care...

Everything You Ever Wanted to Know About...

Absolutely nothing, because we really don't care...

Everything You Ever Wanted to Know About...

Absolutely nothing, because we really don't care...

Everything You Ever Wanted to Know About...

Absolutely nothing, because we really don't care...

Everything You Ever Wanted to Know About...

Absolutely nothing, because we really don't care...

Everything You Ever Wanted to Know About...

Absolutely nothing, because we really don't care...

Everything You Ever Wanted to Know About...

Absolutely nothing, because we really don't care......

Everything You Ever Wanted to Know About...

Absolutely nothing, because we really don't care...

Everything You Ever Wanted to Know About...

Absolutely nothing, because we really don't care...

Everything You Ever Wanted to Know About...

Absolutely nothing, because we really don't care....

Everything You Ever Wanted to Know About...

Absolutely nothing, because we really don't care...

Everything You Ever Wanted to Know About...

Absolutely nothing, because we really don't care...

Everything You Ever Wanted to Know About...

Absolutely nothing, because we really don't care...

Everything You Ever Wanted to Know About...

Absolutely nothing, because we really don't care...

Everything You Ever Wanted to Know About...

Absolutely nothing, because we really don't care...

Everything You Ever Wanted to Know About…

Absolutely nothing, because we really don't care…

Everything You Ever Wanted to Know About...

Absolutely nothing, because we really don't care...

Everything You Ever Wanted to Know About...

Absolutely nothing, because we really don't care...

Everything You Ever Wanted to Know About...

Absolutely nothing, because we really don't care...

Everything You Ever Wanted to Know About...

Absolutely nothing, because we really don't care...

Everything You Ever Wanted to Know About...

Absolutely nothing, because we really don't care...

Everything You Ever Wanted to Know About...

Absolutely nothing, because we really don't care....

Everything You Ever Wanted to Know About....

Absolutely nothing, because we really don't care...

Everything You Ever Wanted to Know About...

Absolutely nothing, because we really don't care...

Everything You Ever Wanted to Know About...

Absolutely nothing, because we really don't care...

Everything You Ever Wanted to Know About...

Absolutely nothing, because we really don't care...

Everything You Ever Wanted to Know About...

Absolutely nothing, because we really don't care...

Everything You Ever Wanted to Know About...

Absolutely nothing, because we really don't care...

Everything You Ever Wanted to Know About...

Absolutely nothing, because we really don't care...

Everything You Ever Wanted to Know About...

Absolutely nothing, because we really don't care...

Everything You Ever Wanted to Know About...

Absolutely nothing, because we really don't care...

Everything You Ever Wanted to Know About...

Absolutely nothing, because we really don't care...

Everything You Ever Wanted to Know About...

Absolutely nothing, because we really don't care...

Everything You Ever Wanted to Know About...

Absolutely nothing, because we really don't care...

Everything You Ever Wanted to Know About...

Absolutely nothing, because we really don't care...

Everything You Ever Wanted to Know About…

Absolutely nothing, because we really don't care…

Everything You Ever Wanted to Know About…

Absolutely nothing, because we really don't care…

Everything You Ever Wanted to Know About…

Absolutely nothing, because we really don't care…

Everything You Ever Wanted to Know About...

Absolutely nothing, because we really don't care...

Everything You Ever Wanted to Know About...

Absolutely nothing, because we really don't care...

Everything You Ever Wanted to Know About...

Absolutely nothing, because we really don't care...

Everything You Ever Wanted to Know About...

Absolutely nothing, because we really don't care...

Everything You Ever Wanted to Know About...

Absolutely nothing, because we really don't care...

Everything You Ever Wanted to Know About...

Absolutely nothing, because we really don't care...

Everything You Ever Wanted to Know About...

Absolutely nothing, because we really don't care...

Everything You Ever Wanted to Know About...

Absolutely nothing, because we really don't care...

Everything You Ever Wanted to Know About...

Absolutely nothing, because we really don't care...

Everything You Ever Wanted to Know About...

Absolutely nothing, because we really don't care...

Everything You Ever Wanted to Know About...

Absolutely nothing, because we really don't care...

Everything You Ever Wanted to Know About...

Absolutely nothing, because we really don't care...

Everything You Ever Wanted to Know About...

Absolutely nothing, because we really don't care...

Everything You Ever Wanted to Know About….

Absolutely nothing, because we really don't care…

Everything You Ever Wanted to Know About...

Absolutely nothing, because we really don't care…..

Everything You Ever Wanted to Know About…

Absolutely nothing, because we really don't care…

Everything You Ever Wanted to Know About...

Absolutely nothing, because we really don't care...

Everything You Ever Wanted to Know About…

Absolutely nothing, because we really don't care…

Everything You Ever Wanted to Know About...

Absolutely nothing, because we really don't care...

Everything You Ever Wanted to Know About...

Absolutely nothing, because we really don't care...

Everything You Ever Wanted to Know About...

Absolutely nothing, because we really don't care...

Everything You Ever Wanted to Know About…

Absolutely nothing, because we really don't care…

Everything You Ever Wanted to Know About...

Absolutely nothing, because we really don't care...

Absolutely nothing at all, because we really don't care...

Made in the USA
Columbia, SC
26 December 2022